Political Campaigns and Social Media

A Winning Combination

Table of Contents

There's too much money in politics, and it skews the system. The Internet and social network revolution is going to help level the playing field.

Chapter 1. Introduction

Dive into the unmatched vigor of a groundbreaking Special Report: Political Campaigns and Social Media: A Winning Combination. Navigate the captivating intersection of politics and technology, a novel frontier where charismatic candidates and savvy social media strategies conspire to sway the scales of democracy. Irrespective of your political interests or tech savvy-ness, this engaging report promises an enrichening journey, packed with vibrant illustrations, intriguing case studies, and insightful discussions. Step inside, and unveil the pivotal role of social media platforms in transforming political discourse and shaping democratic outcomes. This lively Special Report is not only a treasury of knowledge, but an opportunity to decipher the underlying mechanics of your favorite social media channels amidst political campaigns. As if this isn't irresistible enough, be warned that the Special Report is as unputdownable as your favourite political thriller, guaranteed to leave you enriched and wanting more! So, why wait? Give in to the call and equip yourself today with this illuminating compendium!

Chapter 2. The Advent of Social Media in Politics

Political landscapes the world over have long been influenced by various communication channels, from the spoken word to printed newspapers, radio broadcasts, television media, and now the expansive realm of the internet. With the new millennium, the world witnessed the birth of social media — a milestone in the evolution of communications technology. The first section of this chapter will further delve into the inception of social media, tracing its historical roots and how it managed to swiftly ensnare the public's attention, thereby laying the foundation for its use in political campaigns.

2.1. The Birth of Social Media and its Steep Growth Curve

Social media, as we understand it today, is a relatively new phenomenon. The turn of the century marked the beginning of this digital revolution. In 2004, Mark Zuckerberg and his Harvard roommates birthed Facebook. Initially intended as a platform for networking among college students, Facebook's gargantuan success soon saw its expansion, capturing the public's intrigue across the globe. However, it was the advent of Twitter in 2006 that originally authorised the rapid dissemination of short-form content, propelling social media into the limelight.

In 2010, Instagram was introduced, manifesting a unique melding of image and text that allowed for creative, visually centered communication. Over the years, various other platforms entered the scene, ushering in a new era for digital communication. LinkedIn connected professionals, Pinterest functioned as a digital scrapbook, Snapchat revolutionised storytelling, YouTube brought independent video content to the fore, and conversational sites like Reddit found their place.

Emerging amidst the digital transition, these platforms collectively transformed the way people connected, imparted information, and engaged with brands, movements, and — you guessed it — politics. A mere decade into the millennium and social media was already an established part of the world's communication fabric.

2.2. Politicians Meet Social Media - A Liaison of Necessity

It did not take long for politicians to grasp the immense potential of these platforms. They clocked their gigantic reach and impressive engagement and swiftly began shaping their digital strategies. As early as the 2008 US Presidential race, then-Senator Barack Obama harnessed the power of social media, employing it as a pivotal tool in his campaign strategy. His novel approach to fundraising and grassroots organizing via social media channels proved to be a gamechanger — both for his campaign and the political sphere at large.

In fact, many pundits and political analysts consider Obama's victory as the start of a new era in political campaigning, one defined by the power of the internet and social media. This marked the beginning of social networks and digital platforms being repurposed as socio-political stages, vibrating with activism, debate, and genuine emotional connection.

Indeed, social media offered a new, unfiltered, and interactive platform for politicians to communicate directly with the populace — thus augmenting their reach, engaging with voters, and indeed, swaying public opinion.

2.3. Revisiting Traditional Political Campaigning in the Light of Social Media

Social media platforms fundamentally disrupted traditional political campaigning. Prior to social media's advent, political campaigning was a one-way street — from politicians to the public. Regular folks were primarily passive recipients of political messaging, with only limited venues for interacting directly with the political establishment.

However, social media, with its open, interactive nature, changed this dynamic entirely. Suddenly, ordinary citizens had a chance to directly voice their concerns, ask questions, and respond to political announcements. This interactive feature of social media propelled a significant shift in political discourse and the electoral process, seeding the roots for a new type of politics — one where the audience-voters play an active role in shaping the campaign narrative.

2.4. Social Media and the Global Political Landscape

With all of this in mind, the presence and the rapidly expanding influence of social media are not constrained just to Western democracies. Its impact reverberates around the globe, altering the way political campaigns are conducted in various countries.

From the Arab Spring movements, where social media functioned as catalyst and sounding board, to more recent examples like the Chennai floods in India, where the platforms facilitated citizen-led responses and communication, we witness the undeniable influence of social media. Both developed and developing nations have had their politics revolutionised, their voices amplified, and their democratic process reshaped. From grassroots campaigning to strategic geopolitical manoeuvring, social media is now wedded to politics.

This chapter merely scratches the surface of social media's complex and increasingly pervasive role in the political field. The depth of its impact and the multiplicity of its ramifications is expounded in subsequent chapters.

Chapter 3. Impact of Social Media on Political Campaigns: A New Era

For as long as we can remember, the arena of politics has been a theater of operations where candidates reached out to the masses through public speeches, printed materials, and with the advent of radio and television, broadcast media. The arrival of the Internet heralded a new era, and with it, a new dimension called social media debuted on the political stage. It brought about significant shifts in the art and strategy of political campaigns.

3.1. Winds of Change: The Internet and Politics

The Internet revolutionized the way information travels. It redefined the dynamics of communication and brought the globe together like never before. But above all, it changed the rules of the game in politics. No longer were citizens just passive receivers; they could now instantly react, comment, or share information, and even take part in political dialogue. Political campaigns, once a one-way broadcasting activity, morphed into a dynamic two-way interaction with the potential to reach millions of homes around the globe.

3.2. Scene Stealer: Social Media's Grand Entry

If the arrival of the Internet was a gust of change, the advent of social media was nothing short of a torrent. Social media platforms like Facebook, Twitter, and Instagram soon became the new town square where people congregated, shared ideas, and held discussions. This brought in the next revolution in political campaigns. These platforms offered a level of interactivity and reach that was unprecedented in the history of political canvassing. They allowed direct connections between the politicians and the people — making way for a personal bonding instrumental to gaining voter trust and buffing candidate appeal.

A case in point can be the 2008 U.S presidential elections, where a young Democratic nominee, Barack Obama, embraced social media to reach out to the then largely untapped youth electorate. He built an engaging persona on platforms like Twitter and Facebook, directly interacting and sharing policy ideals. This strategy turned out to be a game-changer, leading to his ultimate victory and setting a precedent for social media's use in political campaigns.

3.3. Social Media: A New Battleground

Unlike traditional mediums, where politicians deliver messages carefully crafted by their campaign managers, social media offers them the chance to present a more human side, demonstrating personal beliefs, values, and even their sense of humor. This ability to humanize politicians has brought a noticeable shift in favorability and public perception towards them.

Social networking platforms have not only enabled politicians to reach the masses substantially but also allowed them a peek into their constituents' lives and beliefs. The personal data shared by users on these platforms provide invaluable demographic data and insights into public opinions, helping politicians tailor their campaign messages better.

3.4. Grassroots 2.0: Mobilization and Fundraising

Beyond communication, social media platforms also serve as robust tools for campaign mobilization and fundraising. Earlier, political funding came largely from corporations and wealthy donors. However, social media facilitates the pooling of small donations from a large number of individuals — leading to what can be called 'crowd-funded' campaigns. This route not only enlarges the donor base but also reflects the personal stake and sentiment of a more comprehensive demographic towards the candidate or the party.

3.5. A Reality Check: Not All Roses

While the rise of social media as an integral part of political campaigns has undeniably democratized information access and dissemination, it also comes with its set of concerns. The most significant being the spread of misinformation. The advent of fake news and systematic misinformation campaigns have endangered the integrity of democratic processes. Blurred lines of privacy with the gathering of personal data for micro-targeting is another issue haunting this digital era of political campaigning.

In conclusion, the impact of social media on political campaigns is profound and transformative. Not only has it reshaped how politicians connect with their constituents, but it has also restructured the traditional hierarchical structure of politics. It has provided an avenue for a more intimate and direct connection between the politicians and the public, leading to more personalized campaigns. Nevertheless, the challenges it brings also need due consideration and addressal to ensure transparent and honest political discourse in the foreseeable future.

Chapter 4. The Strategy: Crafting Successful Social Media Political Campaigns

The transformation of the political landscape through social media is not an accidental occurrence but rather a result of carefully crafted strategies and meticulous execution. This chapter dives into the fascinating world of political campaigns on social media, illuminating the methods, tactics, and blueprints that make a campaign successful.

4.1. The Blueprint of Social Media Strategy

Social media has breathed new life into political campaigns. But what is it that makes some campaigns stand out while others recede into the digital void? The secret lies in crafting a robust strategy. A clear blueprint should be the cornerstone of any successful social media political campaign. This includes identifying the target audience, determining the appropriate message, choosing the appropriate platform, understanding the algorithm, planning for the campaign's timing and frequency, and managing the budget for advertising.

Social media, with all of its intricacies, offers an unprecedented level of granularity in target audience selection. Utilizing audience analytics, political campaigners can tailor messages to cater to the interests and concerns of specific demographic groups. These messages can range from policy stances to campaign updates, all presented through bespoke video content, infographics, and intelligent copywriting.

4.2. Understanding and Manipulating the Algorithm

While traditional media has generally allowed for a straightforward presentation of messages, social media presents its own set of challenges and opportunities. These platforms use complex algorithms to determine what content should be shown to a particular user. Success lies not merely in understanding these algorithms, but also in manipulating them to work in favor of the campaign.

To master the algorithm, campaign strategists must learn to produce content that sparks engagement. Highly shared, liked, or commented content is more likely to be boosted by the algorithm. Adding to this, the timing and frequency of posts play a crucial role in staying on the radar of the target audience. Consequently, thought needs to be given to when and how often a campaign posts updates.

4.3. The Role of Paid Advertising

Despite the potential for organic growth, paid advertising holds a significant place in social media campaigns. It offers the advantage of guaranteed exposure and is particularly effective for expanding reach and driving engagement amongst new audience segments. A careful balance of organic content and paid promotions can optimize resources for clear, measurable, and impactful electioneering.

4.4. Subtleties of Each Platform

The choice of platforms also considerably influences campaign strategy. For instance, Twitter's character limit nudges campaigns to deliver concise, punchy messages. Instagram, a more visually centric platform, necessitates engaging visual content — photographs, illustrations, infographics, and short videos. Facebook combines the merits of text and visual content but requires an understanding of its unique algorithm. LinkedIn, although less commonly used for political campaigns, can be an effective tool for more serious and policy-driven communication. Hence, the strategy must flex across different platforms based on their distinct natures.

4.5. Rise of Feedback and Interactivity

Another distinctive feature of social media campaigns is the two-way communication it affords, turning passive receivers of messages into active participants. This interactivity enables real-time feedback, which can and should be used to tweak strategies or correct course if needed. It also fosters a sense of inclusion and engagement amongst voters, bolstering their emotional investment and loyalty to the candidate or party.

4.6. Case Study: Using Strategy Effectively

An example illustrating strategy well-implemented is Barack Obama's 2008 Presidential campaign. With the understanding that younger and more internet savvy Americans were a crucial demographic, the campaign leveraged social media in unprecedented ways. They identified key platforms of the era (Facebook and Twitter), and used them effectively for mobilization of voters, fundraising, and presenting the candidate's persona. In addition, a thoughtfully deployed grassroots strategy utilized user-generated content, lending authenticity and a personal touch to the campaign.

As this chapter shows, social media can be an extraordinarily powerful tool in politics, displaying its capacity to profoundly reshape and steer political campaigns towards success. But harnessing this power requires a deeply considered, well-executed strategy, keeping in mind the ever-evolving dynamics of the digital landscape. It's no longer about merely being present on social media, but about how nimbly and deftly one navigates the complex online maze that could ultimately determine the outcome of the race.

Chapter 5. The Tools of Influence: Facebook, Twitter, and Beyond

Social media's ascent to prominence has, in large part, been fueled by its increasingly prevalent role in politics. Just as politics, in general, provide the foundational underpinnings of our societal framework, much of the socio-political discourse today is driven by the mechanics of social media platforms, particularly Facebook and Twitter, and goes far beyond.

5.1. The Supremacy of Facebook and Twitter

When it comes to social media platforms wielding political influence, two names stand out - Facebook and Twitter. Their impact on politics is magnified by their vast user base, robust algorithms, and the potential to disseminate information rapidly and widely. Facebook, with its over two billion active users, offers politicians an open avenue for micro-targeting, a technique that capitalizes on personal data to deliver tailored messages to specific demographic segments. Twitter, on the other hand, with its fast-paced timeline and 280 character limit, swiftly propagates political viewpoints, making it a favorite platform for political figures and a crucial tool for political discourse.

Strategic use of Facebook can foster a sense of personal connection between politicians and their constituents. Politicians can use the platform's variety of features - regular posts, Facebook Live, polls, to showcase their authenticity, relatability, and political prowess, thereby enticing voters and boosting their overall public image.

Twitter's real-time nature lends itself well to real-time commentary. Politicians use the platform to engage with constituents, respond to political developments quickly, and shape public sentiment. A well-timed, incisive tweet can act as a powerful tool, perhaps sometimes even more potent than traditional media channels.

While politicians stand to gain significantly from these platforms, they also need to remain vigilant about potential fake news, disinformation, and privacy issues.

5.2. Beyond Facebook and Twitter: Other Social Media Tools

While Facebook and Twitter indisputably hold significant shares of the political social media landscape, they are not the only contenders. Politicians and political campaigners are refining their strategies to exploit a medley of social media platforms proficiently.

Instagram, with its visual appeal, enables politicians to display a more personalized side. Politicians frequently leverage Instagram stories, IGTV, and Instagram Live to share behind-the-scenes footage or respond to queries in real-time.

YouTube, another critical platform, serves as a hub for political campaign ads, speeches, and townhall meetings. Candidates can manipulate YouTube's advanced targeting options to circulate their message selectively.

LinkedIn, the professional networking site, is an often under-utilized but powerful asset. Politicians can use LinkedIn to discuss economic policies, create job proposals, industry insights, and cater to their professional demographic.

Finally, newer platforms like Snapchat and TikTok offer younger demographics. Using these platforms, politicians can deliver bite-sized, effectively tailored content to charm their younger constituents.

5.3. Crafting a Multifaceted Social Media Strategy

For a social media campaign to be effective, it requires a meticulous approach. This includes dedicating time to understanding each platform's norms, the dynamics of content sharing, knowing the demographics of each platform, and crafting an approach accordingly.

Compelling narratives and engaging content form the backbone of any social media political campaign. Content must resonate with audiences and impel them to share, thereby extending reach and influence. Understanding algorithmic preferences of different platforms can help politicians achieve greater visibility and engagement.

Integration across platforms is another strategy often employed. For politicians, ensuring their message aligns across all platforms creates a stronger brand image.

It's equally critical to track and analyze performance metrics. Reliable data allows politicians and their teams to tweak strategies for maximum efficiency, whether that translates to gaining more followers, creating more engaging content, or handling crisis management.

5.4. Conclusion: The Power of Social Media Tools

Social media plays a pivotal role in political campaigns and governance. As platforms evolve, they provide an array of tools for politicians and political campaigners to influence voters and shape political discussions. Implementing a comprehensive social media strategy, recognizing the strengths and functionalities of each platform, can determine whether a politician successfully navigates the dynamic political landscape or fades into oblivion. However, they also surface challenges such as disinformation, echo chambers, and privacy breaches, marking the need for responsible usage and conscious engagement.

Chapter 6. Case Studies: Successful Campaigns and Their Impact

Case studies have always been cornerstones of academic literature and scientific exploration. Through deconstructed, expert evaluation of practical examples, they offer insights that transcend theoretical rhetoric driving us closer to the core of the subject matter. As such, in this section, we shall delve deep into three notable instances of successful political campaigns and how they effectively deployed the dynamism of social media channels to influence, incite and ultimately, inspire desired democratic outcomes.

6.1. Barack Obama's 2008 Presidential Campaign

In the annals of political history, Obama's 2008 Presidential Campaign stands as a pioneering triumph of social media leveraging. His campaign team did not merely use the digital world as an alternative billboard but as a space to foster close-knit grassroot communities and birth an innovative, constituent-focused approach to political communication.

Social media giants, Facebook and Twitter were still fledglings in the political landscape and Obama's daring play to utilise these platforms to the fullest astounded many traditionalists. He had over 2 million Facebook supporters, almost 120,000 followers on Twitter before election day, marking a substantial digital lead over his rival. Furthermore, the campaign launched a tailored social media platform, "my.BarackObama.com," that facilitated organization, events, and fundraising.

This bold strategy positively reverberated throughout his campaign netting in a technological advantage reflected in the voting booths across America. Obama's campaign was not merely a fantastic demonstration of the newborn prowess of social media, but it also offered a groundbreaking strategy-template for future politicians.

6.2. Narendra Modi's 2014 General Election Campaign

Crossing over to the bustling democracy of India, we find the charismatic leader Narendra Modi, who razed traditional limits and deployed an exhaustive social media campaign during the 2014 General Elections. The campaign was a paradigm shift for Indian politics, previously restricted to ground rallies and traditional media.

Modi's team comprehensively employed Twitter, Facebook, and homegrown social platforms such as NaMo app. His Twitter account became a hub of political discourse, used to communicate directly with citizens, highlight policy initiatives, and rally support during the campaign. Live streams of his rallies on YouTube coupled with interactive 'Chai Pe Charcha' (discussions over tea) sessions on other platforms enhanced public engagement.

Stunningly, Modi's digital presence enormously aided in the formation of a near-absolute majority government in a predominantly multiparty system. The finite intricacies of Modi's social media strategy tilt the scales of electoral battles, ingraining the influence of these platforms in India's political tableau.

6.3. Donald Trump's 2016 Presidential Campaign

Donald Trump's bombastic 2016 Presidential Campaign presents a drastic paradigm shift in leveraging social media, pushing boundaries of previous norms and harnessing the power of immediacy and virality. Trump's approach centered around Twitter, a platform he utilized with unmatched ferocity to set narratives, engage supporters, and even incite controversy.

The election campaign saw an unfiltered Trump, whose tweets garnered massive attention, accruing millions of likes, retweets, and replies. Though unconventional, the seemingly unbridled approach led to expansive media coverage and constant spotlight, arguably contributing to Trump's eventual electoral victory.

In summary, Trump's campaign, notwithstanding its controversy, added another layer to the evolving interface of politics and social media. It redefined norms and established the profound power and potential of social media platforms as conversation-shapers, indirectly forcing us to question and duly ponder upon the ethos surrounding political discourse in digital spaces.

In evaluating these case studies, a common thread surfaces - social media has swiftly transformed from being a mere campaign adjunct to an instrumental factor in shaping election outcomes. Each case shows unique dimensions of social media deployment, offering valuable lessons and cues for future campaigns. The underpinning theme, however, remains the effective harnessing of the interactive, viral, and uniquely relatable power of social media, a testament to this digital age. The profound and ingenious impact of these campaigns shapes political strategizing, pushing towards an ever-tightening bond between politics and social media.

Chapter 7. Understanding the Demographics: Who is the Political Social Media Audience?

Begin your understanding of this chapter with the fundamental acknowledgment that the audience of political social media campaigns is not a singular, homogenous entity, but rather, an amalgamation of distinctly diverse groups. Each of these groupings is a reflection of their respective demographics, ideologies, and regional affiliations — but, also, of their interests, behavioral patterns, and social media habits. Collective awareness and understanding of these factions, their characteristics, and their ways of consuming information is vital for any candidate or party wishing to craft a successful political campaign on social media platforms.

7.1. Unraveling the Complex Fabric of Social Media Audiences

Analyzing the demographics of a social media audience forms the cornerstone of any effective political campaign. Comprehensive comprehension thereof requires a multifaceted approach, encompassing age, gender, socioeconomic status, education level, geography, and ethnicity. Major social media platforms regularly furnish such demographic data to aid more tailored, effective campaigning.

Age, for one, plays a critical role. Younger audiences, predominantly digital natives, might employ platforms like Instagram, Snapchat, and TikTok, while the 25-34 year age group commonly utilizes Facebook. Older demographics, correspondingly, hold sway on platforms like

Twitter and LinkedIn.

But, age is not the sole determinant. Geography, too, plays a significant part; certain platforms might be more popular in specific regions than others. For instance, Facebook enjoys widespread popularity in both urban and rural America, while Instagram skews more toward metropolitan centers.

However, understanding demographics isn't merely about compartmentalization. It lies in appreciating the intersectionality between these categories, thereby comprehending how these audiences consume and interact with political content on social media.

7.2. Platform Specific Demographics: A Closer Look

Each social media platform caters to a specific set of demographics, and understanding this specificity allows for more targeted political campaigns.

Facebook, which is decidedly a platform for the masses, has over 2.7 billion active users worldwide. A Pew Research Center study indicates a near-even gender split among Facebook users, and a large number of daily users spanning diverse age groups and educational backgrounds. This makes Facebook an all-encompassing tool for political engagement and rhetoric.

Twitter, on the other hand, attracts a relatively more educated and affluent audience with a male bias. Its real-time nature as an information sharing and news platform makes it ideal for political debates and conversations. With its potential for real-time engagement, Twitter offers opportunities for both politicians and their constituencies to engage in open dialogue, fostering transparent communication and reciprocate feedbacks.

Instagram and **Snapchat**, with their strong appeal to younger demographics, provide compelling visual narratives, aiding candidates to connect with younger voters in a more personal, less formal way.

7.3. The Intricacies of Behavioral Patterns

Demarking who utilizes what platform represents only half the picture. Equally essential is decoding the habits and behavioral patterns of these users - the when, why, and how of their interaction with political messages on social media.

Younger audiences thrive on image-centric content and engage more with bite-sized political information. Older demographics, conversely, display a penchant for extensive text-based material — policy briefs, thinktank pieces, long-reads — dichotomizing their social media behavior considerably.

Individuals often reshare political posts that align with their beliefs, leading to an echo-chamber effect. Recognizing such patterns, candidates can thus tailor their messages to reinforce pre-established beliefs or challenge narrative biases.

7.4. The Determining Role of Demographics in Political Engagement

Political candidates can leverage the vast trove of demographic and behavioral information available to them to drive more focused engagement. By tailoring campaign messages to the interests, viewpoints, and needs of specific demographic groups, candidates can develop authentic connections that resonate deeply, enhance campaign appeal, stir discussions, and motivate action.

For example, campaigns can leverage the visual appeal of Instagram to communicating complex policy stances or statistics to a younger demographic. Using the conversational nature of Twitter, they can engage in public discussions and debates. Even platforms like LinkedIn can serve as confident vessels for outreach toward professional audiences.

Navigating the seas of demographic variation requires dexterity and understanding, but given its substantial impact on the effectiveness and reach of messages, it's an endeavor worth tackling. This exploration has underlined not just the diversity and complexity of social media users, but also the ways in which political campaigns can, and do, use demographic and behavioral data to deliver more focused, compelling, and relevant messages. This dynamic interplay between politics and social media, therefore, is an evolving narrative, continuously shaping and reshaping the democratic landscape across the globe.

Chapter 8. The Role of Fake News and Fact-Checking in Political Campaigns

In this rich, panoramic discourse, we embark upon the compelling exploration of two crucial pillars dominating the realm of political campaigns in a digitally fueled society—fake news and fact-checking. Herein, we dive deep into how these two counterparts co-exist, interact, and influence the social media landscape in the context of political campaigns.

8.1. Understanding Fake News: The Concept and Its Mechanics

The shadowy terrain of fake news is laden with credulous truths and believable lies aimed at belying the facts. What is fake news exactly? Fake news is factually incorrect or misleading information presented as news. Often it takes the form of stories or rumors that are deliberately fabricated to deceive the reader, to influence their beliefs, or to incite action or inaction based on these mendacious narratives.

The mechanics of fake news operation aren't a bolt out of the blue. Social media platforms, with their billions of users worldwide, facilitate a conducive environment for the rapid dissemination of such information. The reasons are manifold—a blend of human psychology yearning for sensational stories, algorithmic advances promoting more engaging content irrespective of its veracity, and occasionally, malicious parties leveraging these paradigms to drive their personal or political agendas.

8.2. The Scale of Fake News

Grasping the enormity of the fake news phenomenon can be challenging without a close look at some tangible data. Consider the findings of an MIT study that examined around 126,000 stories shared by nearly 3 million Twitter users between 2006 and 2017. Shockingly, it revealed that fake news spreads six times faster than factual news. This alarming fact clearly showcases the scale and speed enhancing the propagation of fake news, making its influence hard to ignore or underestimate.

8.3. Fake News: A Potent Tool in Political Campaigns

In the arena of political campaigns, fake news has emerged as a potent tool, capable of manipulating public sentiment, sowing discord, and in extreme cases, even tilting the scales of electoral outcomes. Predominantly, the misleading narratives target corruption scandals, controversial policies, and personality assassinations, all crucial aspects that can steer voter perception.

Throughout political history, there have been instances where fake news has played a significant role. The 2016 U.S. presidential election is a prime example where torrents of fake news flooded the informational landscape, with both the candidates becoming targets as well as supposed propagators of such misleading information.

8.4. Fact-Checking: The Sentinel Against Fake News

Fact-checking emerges as the silver lining in this fake news laden cloud, serving as a crucial mechanism that seeks to ensure accuracy and uphold public trust in media reporting, particularly in the highly charged environment of political campaigns. It involves scrutinizing statements or claims, tracing their origins, and validating them with primary sources or established facts.

8.5. The Rise of Fact-Checking Organizations

In the wake of growing fake news infestation, the number of fact-checking organizations has proliferated worldwide. These organizations work tirelessly to debunk false information and provide the public with verifiable information. From PolitiFact to FactCheck, these organizations meticulously sift through vast data piles, using a blend of investigative journalism, data analysis, and in some cases, community help, saving the internet strata from drowning in a sea of misinformation.

8.6. Fact-Checking in the Era of Social Media Political Campaigns

While fact-checking is a time-honored journalistic practice, its importance has been amplified in the realm of social media-driven political campaigns. Digital platforms like Twitter and Facebook are awash with an incessant stream of claims and counter-claims, demanding a proactive, robust fact-checking process. For instance, Facebook has initiated third-party fact-checking programs, signaling its impetus on countering false information.

8.7. The Challenges of Fact-Checking

That said, fact-checking isn't devoid of challenges. The sheer volume of content to be evaluated, the rapid pace of information dissemination, and often, the intricate subtleties of language, context, and semantics make it a daunting task. Moreover, the backlash from debunked parties can sometimes escalate to unanticipated hostility, legal suits, or threats.

This chapter concludes at an intersection of caution and vigilance. Fake news, despite its drawbacks, continues to mar the otherwise promising landscape of social media political campaigning. It challenges our shared reality, incites political polarization, and undermines democracy. On the contrary, fact-checking underlines our collective endeavor to reinforce the fortification of truth in the world's political discourse. Together, they underline a dynamically evolving symbiosis, defining the modern face of political campaigns. As our journey further unfurls into the deep recesses of this intriguing confluence of politics and technology, the takeaway hallmarks the call for awareness, insightfulness, and engagement in our digitally shared, politically active spaces.

Chapter 9. How Social Media Shapes Public Opinion and Voting Behavior

The dawn of the digital age has significantly overhauled the way information is disseminated and consumed, presenting an array of implications particularly pertinent to the sphere of public opinion formation and voter behavior. In the heart of this revolution lie social media platforms that are increasingly flexing their muscles to shape what people know, discuss, and believe about political issues to ultimately influence their voting behaviors. This chapter painstakingly dissects this complex interplay, offering an in-depth analysis of how social media hones its malleability to mold public opinion and sway voting patterns.

9.1. The Power of Social Media in Dissemination of Information

At its core, social media serves as an infinite repository of incessantly updating information, including political ideologies, manifestos, and debates, making it an incredibly potent tool for political discourse. These platforms are now the stage for political campaigns, debates, and interactions, saturation points where differing ideas converge, collide or coalesce. The sheer speed, volume, and reach with which political narratives spread across these platforms exert substantial influence on its consumer's political beliefs and behaviors.

9.2. The Rise of Online Public Sphere

Social media has ignited a paradigm shift, transforming from mere communication tools to vibrant digital public spheres. Thanks to its democratized structure, citizens engage in political debates, voice dissent, or call for reforms, an empowering process that shapes the discourse and potentially alters voting behavior.

9.3. The Echo Chamber Effect

Paradoxically, the very tools that promise to democratize information dissemination often end up having a polarizing effect due to the creation of 'echo chambers' or 'filter bubbles'. Algorithms used by social media platforms often show users content aligning with their existing beliefs, which can skew perceptions and play a critical role in influencing voting decisions, often leading to a lack of diverse political knowledge.

9.4. The Importance of Peer Influence: Online Social Norms

Perhaps one of the most compelling facets of social media's impact on politics is the substantial influence of peers. People's voting decisions are susceptible to the opinions, behaviors, and approvals of their social media peers. Thus, social conformity driven by online social norms can not only reshape public opinion but steer voting behavior.

9.5. The Role of Virality

One crucial attribute of the digitally interconnected landscape is the virality factor, where content can spread like wildfire across diverse demographics with the right impetus, such as a trending hashtag or a sensational piece of news. This mechanism not only shapes public opinion but could also sway voters in favor of or against a candidate.

9.6. Microtargeting: The Customization of Political Communication

With data-driven insights, social media platforms allow political campaigns to engage in 'microtargeting'—tailoring messages to individual voters based on their beliefs, concerns, geographical location, or demographic characteristics. This personalization of political content is playing an increasingly profound role in shaping public opinion and voting behavior.

9.7. The Impact of Fake News

A darker side effect of the digital public sphere's emergence is the proliferation of 'fake news'. Deliberately misleading or false information is often diffused via social media, tainting public opinion, and sowing discord. The extent to which this phenomenon impacts voting behavior is a topic of active research and debate.

9.8. Influencer Politics: Celebrities and Public Figures in the Digital Landscape

High-profile individuals, celebrities, and influencers often wield their considerable social media presence to espouse political views, given their massive follower base. The political conversations initiated or amplified by them can have a substantial bearing on public opinion and voter behavior.

9.9. Conclusion: A Brave New World of Political Discourse

We are standing at an exciting crossroads, a juncture where politics and social media have become inseparable synonyms. As we progress into the future, social media's pivotal role in shaping political landscapes will only grow more profound, impacting public opinion and determining electoral outcomes. Nevertheless, it is imperative for these digital platforms, policymakers, and society as a whole to understand, address, and mitigate the potential pitfalls associated with this unassuming yet transformative phenomenon.

In essence, this chapter served as a deep-sea dive into the ocean of social media politics, aiming to elucidate the intricate relationship between social media, public opinion, and voting behavior. There is undoubtedly still much to uncover, many nuances to disentangle but it's clear that these digital platforms continue to exert their influence, essentially revolutionizing the dynamics of the democratic process.

Chapter 10. The Dark Side: Data Privacy, Security, and Social Media Politics

As we step into the labyrinth of political landscapes dotted with the pulsating technology of social media, it becomes incumbent upon us to uncover the shrouded contours of a seemingly innocuous realm. It is here that we begin our journey, bearing a torch of scrutiny to illuminate the dim, unsettling alleys of the dark side: the contentious issues of data privacy, security, and the role of social media in politics.

10.1. The Enigmatic Dance of Data Privacy and Politics

Our expedition commences at the fragile juncture of data privacy and politics, a point where two worlds collide. Personal data, the lifeblood of social media platforms, once revered as the custodian of digital identities, finds itself at the crossroads: coveted by political campaigns for the wealth of insights, yet relentlessly pursued by privacy advocates for safeguarding the rights of individuals. The social media user, often oblivious to the multitude, finds themselves turned into a mere data point, a unit in the vast trove of big data where political strategists and data scientists delve deep to extract patterns, predilections, and propensities, wielding this power to fashion and direct messages. The contentious sinew connecting politics with personal data incites numerous debates, radiating ripples throughout the democratic tapestry.

10.2. Navigating the Chasm: Cybersecurity and Politics

Following the murky trails of data privacy, we stumble upon the cavernous chasm of cybersecurity. Here, we delve into an intricate symphony of code and cyberspace, where invisible threats lurk in the shadows, striking when least expected. Political campaigns rely heavily on digital platforms, collating reams of data that bear witness to vulnerabilities, open to exploitation by nefarious elements. Breaches, hacks, cyberespionage start whirling around the political narrative, inevitably raising questions about the integrity of data-driven political campaigns. The artful primer draws a vivid sketch of these cybersecurity threats and their detrimental effects on democracy, enriched by real-world instances and expert opinions.

10.3. Weaponizing Social Media: Rise of the Digital Leviathan

Progressing deeper, we cross paths with the specter of weaponized social media. Once envisioned as an idyllic conduit for free thought, opinions, and the democratic spirit, social media's faceted roles have grown more complex and menacing. Malicious actors are revealed, employing an arsenal of digital tools to manipulate, spread disinformation, and sow discord, weaponizing the platforms for political gain. This murky underbelly paints a grim image of the digital architecture that was once considered a cornerstone for political engagement in the democratic spectrum.

10.4. Privacy Rights, State Surveillance, and Social Media

Drawing a breath from the exploration of weaponization, we find ourselves wandering into the tense precincts of privacy rights and state surveillance. Social media, heralded as an egalitarian instrument for freedom of expression, teeters on a dangerous precipice. The pervasive gaze of state-induced surveillance unfurls, centralizing social media as an instrument of control while trampling upon individual privacy rights. Delving into this dystopian landscape, this sub-chapter undertakes a comprehensive analysis of state surveillance and its implications, underpinned by a careful balance between national security and personal freedoms.

10.5. A Clarion Call for Stronger Regulations and Policies

As we near the conclusion, a clarion call resounds, echoing the desperate need for stronger regulations and policies. Social media, bearing the potential for great democratic outreach, is stalked by privacy pitfalls and security breaches. The existing legislation, largely inadequate for managing these complex challenges, is brought under sharp scrutiny. The final leg of our journey offers a compelling argument for robust, agile and adaptive regulations to restore the legitimacy and integrity of the political campaigns inhabiting the social media ecosystem.

After meandering through the intertwined terrains of politics, data privacy, cybersecurity, weaponization of social media, and legal implications, we stand on the periphery of this labyrinth. Enlightened with knowledge and newfound perspectives, we are better equipped to comprehend and navigate the intricate nexus of politics and social media. The dark side of this seemingly innocuous universe eventually reveals itself, doused in the bitter reality of our digital age. As we draw the curtains on this chapter, we find ourselves pondering the delicate balance of leveraging social media for political gains and preserving the democratic sanctity of individual privacy and security.

Chapter 11. Future Perspectives: The Road Ahead for Political Campaigns and Social Media

Our journey of understanding the intricate intertwining between politics and social media in this dynamic digital age brings us to the final yet significant part of this engrossing scholastic voyage - The Future Perspectives and the path that lies in front of political campaigns and social media.

11.1. Engineering a More Engaged and Active Citizenry

Technology and politics, once separate sectors, have fused to form a potent cocktail that influences every democratic process. Looking ahead, social media will continue to be a significant player in the political arena, fostering a more engaged and active citizenry. Whether it's unheard voices finding their place in public discourse or established figures communicating their agendas, social media can democratize the political discourse, breaking down barriers that often marginalize certain groups.

The rise of interactive features, such as live streams or virtual town halls, highlights a growing trend in which politicians can directly engage with voters. This promotes a more participatory democracy, cultivating active citizenship instead of passive spectators. Nevertheless, the impact of these developments must be scrutinized to ensure a healthy democratic dialogue.

11.2. Artificial Intelligence and Political Campaigns

Artificial Intelligence (AI) has made its debut in politics, and it's bound to revolutionize political campaigning on social media. The treasure trove of data on social media platforms enables algorithms to analyze user behavior, interests, and connections, refining political messages to more effectively reach potential voters. However, such promise also harbors perils.

AI-powered systems could be used to manipulate public opinion, exacerbating the spread of misinformation. For instance, "deepfake" technology, where AI is used to create hyper-realistic but wholly false images or videos, can be misused to discredit politicians or mislead voters. Safeguards must be implemented to prevent such abuse, with thoughtful regulation balancing innovation and potential harm.

11.3. The Battle against Disinformation

The past decade has witnessed the rapid growth of fake news, with social media serving as the perfect platform for dissemination. Future strategies for political campaigns on social media must address this issue. Public education campaigns may be launched to bolster digital literacy, promoting discernment of reliable sources and critical assessment of online information.

Moreover, social media platforms are increasingly taking on the responsibility of fact-checking and flagging misleading content. In the future, artificial intelligence may carry the burden of distinguishing fact from fiction at scale, but its accuracy and the implications for free speech are topics of heated debate.

11.4. Role of Data Privacy in Political Campaigns

Progress in data science has given campaigns the capability to micro-target audiences with personalized political advertisements. While this could enhance engagement, it raises significant privacy concerns. Rules around data collection and utilization must be reassessed. Future campaigns may need to strive for transparency, revealing the data collection practices they engage in.

Moreover, social media platforms could refine privacy settings, giving users a greater say in the data they share. Legislations, akin to Europe's General Data Protection Regulation, could be devised globally, offering robust protection for individuals' data.

11.5. Shaping Future Democracy: The Road Ahead

As we look toward the horizon, it becomes evident that social media will continue to shape the political landscape. Politicians, parties, and even governments will have to adapt to this new digital arena, crafting strategies that effectively leverage social media while mitigating its downsides.

Comprehensive digital literacy, stringent data privacy norms, and a concerted fight against disinformation may form the linchpins of future political campaigns on social media. Understanding and embracing this changing dynamism between politics and social media will be key to fostering a robust, inclusive, and participatory democratic process in the future.

There has never been a more exciting time to be at the crossroads of politics and social media. But with great power comes great responsibility. As we move forward into this new era, we must tread thoughtfully, aware of the potential pitfalls as much as the promising opportunities. Our political discourse, our democracy, and even our societal fabric depend on it. For those willing to capitalize on these transformative possibilities while navigating its challenges, the road ahead provides a journey like no other.